STEPHENIE MEYER

ALL ABOUT THE AUTHOR™

STEPHENIE MEYER

TRACY BROWN

ROSEN
PUBLISHING®

New York

For Meghan

Published in 2013 by The Rosen Publishing Group, Inc.
29 East 21st Street, New York, NY 10010

Library of Congress Cataloging-in-Publication Data

Brown, Tracy.
Stephenie Meyer/Tracy Brown.—1st ed.
        p. cm.—(All about the author)
Includes bibliographical references and index.
ISBN 978-1-4488-6936-7 (library binding)
1. Meyer, Stephenie, 1973—Juvenile literature.
2. Authors, American—21st century—Biography—Juvenile literature. I. Title.
PS3613.E979Z636 2012
813'.6—dc23
[B]

2011041698

Manufactured in the United States of America

CPSIA Compliance Information: Batch #S12YA: For further information, contact Rosen Publishing, New York, New York, at 1-800-237-9932.

CONTENTS

Stephenie Meyer—and certainly her famous Twilight series and its beloved characters—are household names all over the world. Her story of a young girl who falls in love with a vampire has captivated readers globally. Meyer's books have been published in nearly fifty countries and have sold more than one hundred million copies worldwide.

The books catapulted Meyer from a quiet life as a housewife in Phoenix, Arizona, to an internationally best-selling author—and all the wealth and fame that come along with that success. According to *Publishers Weekly*, she sold 27.5 million copies of her four Twilight novels in 2008 alone and another 26.5 million copies in 2009.

Hollywood was quick to get in on the Twilight phenomenon, bringing Meyer's stories to the big screen with great success. The film adaptations, created with Meyer's input, proved to be as popular as the books, launching the movie's stars into worldwide recognition almost overnight.

Very few writers ever achieve what Meyer has. She has gripped her readership passionately: readers have become so connected to her characters that people dress up like them, and many have written their own stories about them. It takes a

Meyer is greeted by excited fans at the *New Moon* film premiere held at the Mann Village Theatre on November 16, 2009, in Westwood, California.

remarkable talent to bring a story to life in such a way that the world truly cares what happens to the characters and continues to wonder about them long after finishing the books.

Even with the series completed and the story of Bella and Edward fully told, fans of the books will keep them in their hearts for years to come. For some fans, it goes even further. Cathy Ward, a forty-nine-year-old supermarket worker in Reading, England, is such a die-hard fan that she got her very first tattoo to honor the Twilight saga's characters. She literally covered her back with images of the stars of the Twilight films, Robert Pattinson, Kristen Stewart, and Taylor Lautner. Fortunately, most readers will satisfy themselves by simply rereading the books for years to come!

This book focuses on the woman behind the story. It describes Meyer's writing process, the books and music she credits with inspiring her storytelling, and her life outside of her writing career. Meyer is a true example of where hard work and belief in your story can take you as a writer, and she encourages everyone with a tale to tell just to start writing.

EARLY LIFE

Stephenie Meyer has been, by almost anyone's definition, an overnight success. Coming seemingly out of nowhere, Meyer is now one of the most famous names in publishing. Arguably, her success was partially due to timing. Toward the end of the last decade, with the Harry Potter series coming to a close, the publishing world was hungry for the next big thing. People were searching for the next character and story that would grip readers the way J. K. Rowling's had in her famous stories about a group of brave young wizards. But nobody—not even the author—could have guessed that the next publishing phenomenon, the Twilight series, would stem from

the frantic typing of an inspired housewife in Phoenix, Arizona.

EARLY LIFE

Stephenie Meyer's early life was certainly not predictive of the fantastic success she now enjoys. She had a happy but humble childhood. She was born on December 24, 1973, in Hartford, Connecticut, but she grew up in the more comfortable climate of Phoenix, along with her five siblings, Seth, Emily, Jacob, Paul, and Heidi. Her parents, Stephen and Candy Morgan, were members of the Church of Jesus Christ of Latter-day Saints, and they raised their children with the same beliefs.

Although she was born in Hartford, Connecticut, Meyer grew up in Phoenix, Arizona, shown here lit up at night. Meyer remains an Arizona resident today.

Meyer gets the unusual spelling of her first name—Stephenie—from her father (Stephen + ie). It meant having her named spelled incorrectly most of the time when she was growing up. However, on the Web site Goodreads.com (http://www. goodreads.com), she jokes that today it makes it easier for her to find herself with a Google search— not that Meyer should have any trouble.

The author's childhood was straitlaced, and she still does not drink or smoke. She grew up in a religious Mormon community. It was expected, Meyer recalled in an interview with *Entertainment Weekly*, that she and all of her friends be good girls and that her boyfriends be good boys. She credits growing up in such a positive and happy community with her upbeat and optimistic outlook on the world. She also suggests that her upbringing led her to write about young people who make responsible decisions.

On the Web site Goodreads.com, Meyer describes herself as the "Jan Brady" of her family—the second of three girls in a family that, like *The Brady Bunch*, had six children. Growing up in a large family meant Meyer spent a lot of time helping her parents care for her younger siblings. It also gave Meyer insights into different personality types, which has influenced her characters. She told Linda M. Castellitto of *BookPage* that her siblings often show up in her stories.

EARLY LOVE OF READING

Growing up, Meyer always found adventure, escape, and even romance in books. She was an avid reader—the bookworm of the family—and her house was filled with books that her father encouraged her to read. In a 2009 interview with Robert Sullivan of *Vogue*, she recalled how her father used to sit in the hallway near Stephenie and her siblings' bedrooms and read aloud to them. He read not just children's books but also books for older readers, including fantasy novels such as *The Sword of Shannara* by Terry Brooks. Her father would read until it was bedtime, after which the hooked Stephenie would sneak into the hall and grab the book her father had been reading. She often hid out in the closet, feeling guilty as she read ahead of her siblings.

She credits her mother with inspiring her appreciation for romance in books. Meyer told *Vogue* that she is now obsessed with the love side of stories because her mother kept books by Jane Austen in the house. To this day she enjoys evaluating the relationships of the characters as she soaks up good love stories.

GROWING UP MORMON

While the media, at least initially, focused a great deal on Meyer's Mormon upbringing, in an interview with *USA Today* she insisted that it really wasn't much of a story. It's her religion, period.

But what is the fascination with Mormonism? The Church of Jesus Christ of Latter-day Saints, also known as the Mormon Church, has been portrayed more frequently in recent popular culture. The HBO television series *Big Love* chronicled the life of a man in a Mormon sect who had several wives. The creators of the television show *South Park* have earned acclaim for their hit Broadway musical, *The Book of Mormon*, which describes a young man's experiences as a Mormon missionary in Africa. How accurate are these depictions?

Although polygamy—having multiple spouses—is commonly associated with the church, the vast majority of Mormons are monogamous, having only one partner in marriage. The church is very family-oriented, emphasizing strong ties not only to immediate family but also to relatives in one's extended and multigenerational family. A strict health code prevents the use of tobacco, alcohol, coffee, or tea and calls for adherence to the law of chastity, which bans any sexual relations before marriage or outside of marriage.

Many young male Mormons, in their late teens or early twenties, do indeed serve as missionaries for up to two voluntary years. The Mormon community is primarily based in the Intermountain West, such as in the state of Utah, but the religion is spreading throughout the world, in part through the work of missionaries.

Meyer had a traditional Mormon upbringing, and she embodies many of the church's ideals in her own life—even if her imagination takes her to faraway meadows where young girls fall in love with vampires. So does Meyer consider herself a good representative of her religion? "Being Mormon is part of who I am," Meyer told *Time* magazine. "I try very hard to live the right way, but I don't know that I'm an example. I hate to say, 'Yes, look at me. I'm a good example of being Mormon.' I want to be the best person I can be, so in that respect, maybe I'm a good example."

HIGH SCHOOL DAYS

Meyer went to high school in Scottsdale, Arizona, which she describes on her official Web site (http://www.stepheniemeyer.com) as the Beverly Hills of her home state. Each fall, many of her fellow students would return to school with new Porsches, or even new noses, having had plastic surgery over the summer break. Meyer was not raised to value money and skin-deep beauty, though, and her nose is very much the one she was born with. As for cars, she didn't have one until she was twenty.

According to an article by Olivia Laing in the *Observer*, Meyer was teased as a child growing up

Stephenie Meyer and her husband, Pancho Meyer, arrive at the premiere of the movie *Twilight* in Los Angeles in 2008. As children, Meyer and her husband attended the same church.

in Arizona. Classmates often called her "ghost" on account of her pale skin, and the bullying landed her in counseling. But Meyer had a strong church community and supportive family behind her.

Meyer's family was very connected to their church, and they met many of their friends through church activities. It was at a church gathering that Meyer first "met" a boy named Christiaan Meyer, who went by the nickname Pancho, whom she would eventually marry. On the Web site Goodreads.com, Meyer explains that though they met at age four, they were not childhood sweethearts. "In fact, though we saw each other at least weekly through church activities, I can't recall a single instance when we so much as greeted each other with a friendly wave...When we did eventually get around to exchanging words, sixteen years after our first meeting, it only took nine months from the first 'hello' to the wedding." Still, she and Pancho attended many of the same social gatherings and grew up in the same community, so when they finally did get to know each other better, they already had many memories and experiences in common.

Meyer was an accomplished track runner and a good student, but socially she was a self-confessed wallflower in high school, a mousy girl who was not very popular with the boys, but who had a lot of close girlfriends. When asked by a fan on her official

Students pass a statue of Brigham Young, the second president of the Mormon Church, on the campus of Brigham Young University in Provo, Utah. Meyer majored in English at the university.

Web site why all the male characters in the Twilight books are so attracted to Bella, even though she is described as average-looking, Meyer explains that she modeled some details in the books on her own life, including, it seems, Bella's "averageness." Meyer notes that, ironically, it tends to be the details from her own life in the books that seem the least believable to readers and draw the most criticism— such as Bella winning the hearts of both Edward and Jacob even though she was not drop-dead gorgeous in a traditional sense.

Meyer suggests that Bella's popularity in Forks may be credited to her newness in the small town. "I modeled Bella's move to Forks after my real life move from high school to college," Meyer explains on her Web site, StephenieMeyer.com. "Let me tell you, my stock went through the roof. See, beauty is a lot more subjective than you might think. In Scottsdale, surrounded by Barbies, I was about a five. In Provo [Utah], surrounded by normal people, I was more like an eight. I had dates every weekend with lots of really pretty and intelligent boys (some of whose names end up in my books). It was quite confusing at first, because I knew there was nothing different about me."

COLLEGE BOUND

After graduating from high school in Scottsdale, Arizona, Meyer won a National Merit Scholarship

EMMA.

There was no being displeased with such an encourager, for his admiration made him discern a likeness before it was possible.

LONDON: RICHARD BENTLEY & SON.

This nineteenth-century illustration depicts a scene from Jane Austen's novel *Emma*. Austen is among Meyer's most beloved authors.

and set off to study English at Brigham Young University in Provo, Utah.

Meyer chose to focus her studies on literature, mainly because she enjoyed reading books and did not consider it to be work. She wrote for her college paper, but she did not dabble in writing poems or fiction. In fact, Meyer has had no formal training in creative writing at all, but she is well read and has been a passionate reader throughout her life. Many writers, editors, and teachers will tell you that good readers make good writers. In Meyer's case, her lifelong enjoyment of strong storytelling and her knowledge of genres such as romance and science fiction helped her form her own voice as a writer.

Meyer's all-time favorite writer is Jane Austen, who wrote novels including *Emma* and *Sense and Sensibility* in the early nineteenth century. As for living authors, Meyer is a big fan of science fiction writer Orson Scott Card, with whom she has a few things in common. Card is also an active member of the Church of Latter-day Saints, and he and Meyer attended the same university, although not at the same time.

Meyer graduated from college with a bachelor of arts degree in English in 1995. By this time, she had already tied the knot.

TWO

CHAPTER

THE WIFE AND MOTHER

While visiting home between her junior and senior years at Brigham Young University, the author got to know Pancho Meyer, with whom she'd grown up in the same church community. (Pancho got his nickname from his grandmother, and nobody can remember precisely why. Meyer laments in interviews that it is not a better story.)

Sixteen years after their first meeting, the two went on their first date and hit it off immediately. On the Web site Goodreads. com, Meyer recalls how natural they were in each other's company, right from the start. "Of course, we were able to skip over a lot of the getting-to-know-you parts,"

Stephenie and Pancho Meyer first met in childhood. Their families were active in the same religious community.

she says. "Many of our conversations would go something like this: 'This one time, when I was ten, I broke my hand at a party when...' 'Yeah, I know what happened. I was there, remember?'" In 1994, nine months after getting reacquainted as adults and while she was still a student at Brigham Young University, the two were married. She was just twenty-one years old.

AND BABY MAKES THREE—THEN FIVE

Meyer and her husband set up house in Arizona. She briefly dabbled in working professionally when she was first married, doing administrative jobs such as being a receptionist. Pancho worked as an auditor and earned enough income for the family to survive without Meyer having to work. Once her first son, Gabe, was born, Meyer knew that all

Like the woman in this photo, Meyer wrote in an open office area in the middle of the house so she could keep an eye on the boys.

she wanted to do was stay home and be a mother. Meyer quickly added more children to her family, and she and Pancho now have three boys: Gabe, Seth, and Eli.

Meyer was quite happy as a stay-at-home mom. She did not feel she was missing out on anything in the workplace. She still loved to read, and she appreciated the enrichment that came from having a college education and the university experience. Especially since she was married so young, she believed it was important that she had those years away to discover herself. Now she threw her intelligence and creativity into nurturing and caring for her boys. She made scrapbooks to chronicle their development and childhood experiences, and she designed and sewed fantastic Halloween costumes to set their imaginations alight.

She also read a lot—five or six novels a week. For about six years, she constantly had a baby in one hand and a book in the other. Many would-be writers underestimate the value and necessity of reading to hone your craft. Meyer is a great example of how important it is to be a good reader in order to be a good writer.

MOM BEFORE AUTHOR

Even after she began to write, Meyer was always a mother first and a writer second. She wrote in an

FAMOUS LITERARY MOMS

We live in an exciting time when people, especially women, do not have to limit themselves to choosing family over career, or vice versa. With the freedom and flexibility of the Internet and mobile communications, more and more people are pursuing university degrees and doing professional work from their homes. Authors need little more than a computer and an idea—and perhaps a rich source of reference materials—to fulfill their ambitions. Many famous authors are also mothers, including:

- Isabel Allende is one of Latin America's best-loved female writers. Her novels include *The House of the Spirits*, *The Infinite Plan*, and *The Stories of Eva Luna*.
- Judy Blume is the beloved American author of numerous young adult books, including *Are You There God? It's Me, Margaret* and *Blubber*.
- Ann Brashares is an American author best known for her novel *The Sisterhood of the Traveling Pants* and its sequels.
- J. K. Rowling is the British author of the worldwide publishing phenomenon the Harry Potter series.

open space in the middle of the house rather than closing herself off in a private room, so she could hear and see everything that was going on at home. Meyer wrote her first book while taking care of three

Meyer speaks on stage at the Nokia Theatre in New York City. She encourages anyone with a dream to pursue it, no matter how unlikely it seems.

boys under the age of five. Writing and being a full-time mom is not an easy feat—but her story and her characters possessed her. She typed manically throughout the night or with one hand holding a baby during the day.

Meyer told *Time* magazine that she cannot close a door and write, even if her children are asleep, because she must be somewhere where she can hear them if they need her. She feels better being in the center of things, knowing where everyone is and that everyone is okay.

Even with all her success, Meyer told *USA Today* that first and foremost, she is a stay-at-home Mormon mom to three sons, and that's just how she likes it. "The nice thing is that, 95 percent of the time, I'm just Mom, and we're doing the normal thing," she said. According to Meyer, the most important thing her wealth has afforded her is the ability to stay at home and be with her boys. As she told *Vogue*, she believes the greatest luxury is to be able to take care of your children.

MEYER TO WORKING MOMS: GO FOR IT!

Although Meyer determined that she would be a stay-at-home mother, it does not mean she believes women should not pursue a career and a family. It was Meyer's preference to stay at home and raise her children rather than work outside of the home, but she did not feel conflicted about becoming a writer as soon as she felt the pull.

She encourages women to follow their dreams and to believe they can have it all. According to Meyer, it's just a matter of balance and priorities. "I say go for it," Meyer told *Time*. "I didn't plan to start a career when I did this, and it took a lot of courage to send out those query letters [to literary agents]. If it's something you enjoy, put the determination and will behind it and see what happens."

A LIFE-CHANGING DREAM

On June 2, 2003, Meyer had a dream about a young woman, a regular human, who met a vampire in the woods. The vampire loved the girl but felt conflicted because he had an equally powerful urge to do what vampires normally do to nonvampires: suck her blood, in essence, to kill her. In the dream, an average girl was discussing these problems with the glittery, painfully handsome vampire. They were in love, but there were seemingly too many obstacles.

It was a dream that seemed to come out of nowhere. Meyer dislikes the horror genre, so it wasn't because she was consumed with the idea of monsters. "I'm way too chicken to read horror," she told Gregory Kirschling of *Entertainment Weekly*. It was the kind of dream that you

Vampires have been the subject of countless literary works, but Meyer had never read a vampire novel or watched a movie about the nocturnal creatures before her life-altering dream.

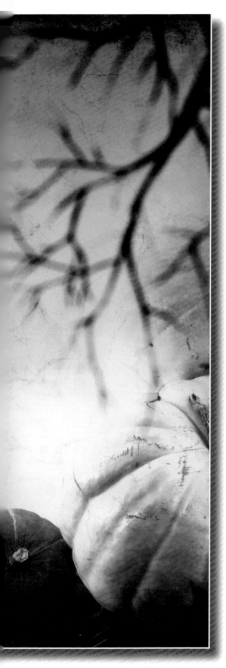

get once in a lifetime, and it unlocked several other stories that lurked in her subconscious.

Meyer could not get the dream out of her head; the next day, Meyer began to write creatively for the first time in her life. She remembers the precise date she began writing—the date she officially became a writer—because it was the same day her children began swimming lessons, affording her a few hours alone to work. She wrote what eventually became chapter 13 of her first book, *Twilight*.

She kept on writing for the next three months. In the time she could find during the day while raising her three boys, and mostly at night while her family slept, Meyer put the dream on paper and finished the complete manuscript, about five hundred pages.

CHARACTERS DRIVE THE PLOT

Meyer is a self-proclaimed character writer. She respects her characters and thinks them all the way through: they have fully developed personalities, vivid backgrounds and experiences, and strong instincts that guide what they do. Her characters' actions and choices drive the plot.

Edward is almost the perfect romantic character. *Seventeen* magazine named Edward one of the best high school boyfriends. Avid fan Libby Scott of New Brunswick, Canada, told Seattlepi.com (http://www.seattlepi.com) that Edward is what every girl wants in a boyfriend: "He's handsome beyond belief, he's polite, he's old-fashioned—he's a true gentleman."

With the character Edward, played by Robert Pattinson in the *Twilight* film and its sequels, Meyer created the perfect vampire boyfriend: he's good-looking, loyal, mysterious, and a gentleman.

When *Newsweek* asked Meyer whether she thinks she has ruined "real men" for young women by presenting this perfect image, Meyer conceded that she probably has, a little bit. But, she added, that might be a good thing. She suggested that although Edward is pure fantasy, there's nothing wrong with having high expectations.

But Edward is also a complex character: he is a handsome, well-meaning vampire who, along with his siblings, has taken a moral stance against drinking human blood. He attempts instead to live off of wild animals. Fighting his natural vampiric instincts is an enormous struggle and one that drives everything Edward does in the books, particularly when it comes to Bella.

This, Meyer said on her Web site, can make Edward as difficult a character to write as he is a boyfriend to hold on to. When writing her first book, *Twilight*, Meyer was not thinking about creating a series but was just writing the story of Edward and Bella as it came to her. When beginning to write the first sequel, *New Moon*, she found she had to question her characters to discover what they would do next.

Meyer had already written a different, unofficial sequel, which she called *Forever Dawn*, and which had more adult themes than the young-adult-oriented *Twilight*. She never intended for it to see the light of day, and instead of publishing it, she gave it to her sister as a birthday gift. When she began writing *New Moon* for publication, she says she went back to Bella's senior year of high school and asked the characters: What happened next? On her official Web site, Meyer explained:

> I should probably mention here that I am not crazy (that I know of), it's just that I am a character writer. I write my stories because of my characters; they are the motivation and the reward. The difficulty with strong, defined characters, though, is that you can't make them do something that is out of character. They have to be who they are and, as a writer, they're often out of your control. As I started plotting New Moon (untitled at that point), it became clear that Edward was Edward, and he would have to behave as only Edward would. And, because of that, Edward was leaving.

Bella's character in *Twilight* was somewhat like Meyer herself. In *New Moon*, the character became more of her own person. When Meyer realized Edward would have to leave Forks in order to protect Bella, Meyer was left with the question: What would Bella do? What do you do when your true

The experiences of Meyer's heroine Bella, played in the movies by actress Kristen Stewart, are loosely based on her own as a teen.

love leaves you? On her Web site StephenieMeyer.com, Meyer said she had to let Bella answer it for herself. Because Meyer is so empathetic to her characters, she often wrote about Bella's pain while experiencing it herself, often writing through her tears. But, she said, the process was fascinating, and Bella sometimes surprised her with her strength and determination.

Meyer knew her characters' personalities and conflicts before she knew their names, and finding names that sounded appropriate took a while. For Edward, she looked to classic romantic literary characters, naming him after Edward Rochester from Charlotte Brontë's *Jane Eyre* and Edward Ferrars from Jane Austen's *Sense and Sensibility*. Meyer gave her female protagonist the name Bella after the name she'd chosen for the daughter she'd never had, Isabella.

MUSIC IS THE BEST MUSE

Picturing Meyer, the happy Mormon wife and mother of three, writing her manuscript while managing her busy suburban life, you might imagine her typing busily in an apron to the white noise of a ticking clock. Not so! Meyer is an alternative music fanatic, and she credits her favorite music with inspiring and motivating her in the writing process.

Meyer listened a great deal to the band Linkin Park while writing the Twilight books. She told *Entertainment Weekly* that the band's music is perfect for fight scenes—the music fuels the momentum as she writes. While writing *New Moon*, Meyer often listened to her favorite band, Muse, which she said is the perfect accompaniment to writing because their songs are so full of angst.

Meyer was consulted on all the soundtracks to her films, and Muse's song "Supermassive Black Hole" was featured on the *Twilight* soundtrack. She told *Rolling Stone*, "It wouldn't feel like this movie was based on something I did without Muse in it." The *Twilight* soundtrack also included the songs "Leave Out All the Rest" by Linkin Park, "Decode" by Paramore, and "Tremble for My Beloved" by Collective Soul. The album won a 2009 American Music Award for Favorite Soundtrack.

Alternative music inspires Meyer as she writes, and the aptly named band Muse is among her all-time favorites. Meyer was thrilled to have the band's music featured in the film adaptations of her work.

CREATING HER CHARACTERS' WORLD

Once Meyer had created her characters, her next task was to put them on the map in a specific setting. Although Meyer's vampires glitter in the sun rather than burn, she believed it made sense to locate them someplace overcast and gray but lush. This was quite a different landscape from Meyer's hometown of Phoenix, which is arid and very sunny.

Meyer began doing Google searches for ideal locations. She discovered that the area of the United States with the most annual rainfall—something anathema to the Arizona native—was the Olympic Peninsula in Washington State. Meyer needed a secluded spot that was surrounded by forest, and she found it in a small town called Forks.

Even the name was perfect, a kind of metaphor for her characters' struggles. In June 2011, Meyer told *Time* magazine that the willingness to choose a different path is a major theme of her books: her characters are constantly confronted with a number of choices in the directions they can take. The message is that when you think you are stuck in life—you can always choose differently, take a different path. In other words, there's always a fork in the road.

Meyer did not visit Forks—she based her ideas on the photographs she was able to find online. She often transported herself to the soggy, misty Northwest while enduring the Phoenix heat during her sons' swimming lessons. In her online research, Meyer also discovered a nearby Native American reservation—the village of La Push, Washington, home to the Quileute tribe. Meyer was fascinated by the Quileute story, and a few fictional members of the tribe became important characters in her books.

VAMPIRE RESEARCH

Vampire stories have been a feature of literature for nearly two hundred years. The first published vampire tale was English author John William Polidori's *The Vampyre*, an 1819 work that was inspired by the life of poet Lord Byron. The best-known classic vampire story is Bram Stoker's *Dracula*, published first in 1897. In modern fiction, Anne Rice wore the vampire authoress crown with her Vampire Chronicles series—at least until Meyer came on the scene.

Meyer created a different breed of vampire. For one thing, vampires traditionally burn in the sun; Meyer's vampires merely glitter. Meyer's vampires are morally bound to preserve human life. Her stories are romantic and suspenseful, but they are not horror shows. So how much research about vampire culture did Meyer do? None.

Because of Meyer's religious upbringing and beliefs, as a young person she never watched R-rated movies. That eliminated many vampire films and other horror films, and Meyer remains uninterested in them today. Her husband loves the vampire film *The Lost Boys*, which Meyer tried to watch but found too creepy. Likewise, she has seen snippets of *Interview with the Vampire* on television, but she has not watched the entire film because she finds it too disturbing.

As for literature, although Meyer does not read horror books, *Dracula* is on her list of books to read—someday. In an interview with Gregory Kirschling of *Entertainment Weekly*, she said she probably ought to have read the book a long time ago and that it is difficult for her to appreciate other authors' vampire stories now. For example, she attempted to read *The Historian* by Elizabeth

This mystical scene in a forest at twilight is similar to the setting of Meyer's Twilight series, which takes place in the real-life town of Forks, Washington.

Kostova but was unable to enjoy it. She told
Kirschling, "I can't read other people's vampires. If
it's too close [to my writing], I get upset; if it's too far
away, I get upset. It just makes me very neurotic."

Meyer did not want to delve into too much
research about vampires while creating her saga.
She already had her vision and basic story line
and was afraid she would stumble onto something
that would alter them. She was creating a world
all her own, and anything that might contradict it

Like many famous romances in literature, the story of Bella and Edward has
captivated fans worldwide. Millions of readers enjoy rooting for the couple, while
others believe that werewolf Jacob is Bella's true love.

would break the spell. She only researched vampires to the degree that Bella did in the series, to learn how to understand her beloved Edward and survive in his world.

What Meyer's books do have in common with other vampire stories is sexual tension. Although her books are squeaky clean—Bella and Edward do little more than kiss—the desire drips off the page. The resistance that Edward maintains to a more physical relationship with Bella makes for steamier romance than more explicit scenes could conjure. For example, Edward tells Bella in *Twilight*, while leaning in close and breathing in her scent: "Just because I'm resisting the wine doesn't mean I can't appreciate the bouquet." The love story has captivated everyone from young girls to middle-aged women.

MANUSCRIPT FINISHED: NOW WHAT?

Meyer completed her first draft of *Twilight* three months after having her fateful dream in June 2003. She had written it purely for her own enjoyment. The characters had consumed her, and their story kept telling itself. Meyer just kept typing. Now with a stack of hundreds of pages before her, she wondered what she should do next.

As an Arizona housewife, Meyer knew nothing about the New York publishing scene, nor did she have any notions—initially—of trying to enter it. She joined a writing club in her local community. Other participants were working on various projects, from greeting cards to journals, but nobody else had a complete manuscript ready to shop around to publishers.

Meyer's older sister, one of the only people who knew that she was busily completing a book, encouraged her to try to get her work published. Meyer jumped into the publishing process completely on her own. She researched literary agents, prepared query letters, formatted and finalized her manuscript, and just went for it. Meyer sent out fifteen letters. She received nine rejections, and five agents never even responded. Then, as Meyer told blogger Cynthia Leitich Smith, she finally got a bite. The place she called her "dream on, Stephenie" agency of choice, Writers House, signed her in October 2003.

It cannot be understated how remarkable this is. Most published authors, and even more unpublished ones, will tell you that it is far from the norm to begin a book in June, complete the first draft, and sign a contract with an industry-recognized literary agent in the span of four to five months. It doesn't happen—except when it does. It can happen for a variety of reasons, though often the quality of the work is not the primary one. Publishers want books with audiences, and it is an agent's job to seek out manuscripts that will appeal to many readers.

Trends in the market at the time can be a major influence on publication, and Meyer's path was in some ways paved by J. K. Rowling. Her Harry Potter series changed the publishing world in several key ways that were important to Meyer's success: Harry Potter showed that kids were willing and able to read long—really long—books and that adults could be drawn into the characters and plots of children's books along with their intended audience. Of course, a writer does not get published without a gripping story, and Meyer had found an agent who believed in her fictional world as much as she did.

Meyer's agent was not wrong in taking a chance on the story of a love-stricken vampire and his determined girlfriend. Just a month later, over Thanksgiving weekend in 2003, Meyer got a life-changing call from her agent: she was being offered a three-book deal from the publisher Little, Brown and Company and a staggering advance of $750,000. Happy Thanksgiving, indeed!

FOUR

CHAPTER

BRINGING HER WORDS TO LIFE

Armed with her impressive book deal, Meyer was still receiving her last few rejection letters from agents. In most cases, to publish a book, two very important things have to happen: first, the author must find an agent who believes in the work enough to put time and effort into selling it to publishers. Then the agent must find an editor who believes in the work enough to purchase and publish the book. Not all agents and editors who read Meyer's manuscript felt it would be a success. However, aspiring authors should remember that an author really needs only one agent and one editor to back what he or she is doing.

On her Web site StephenieMeyer.com, Meyer recalls that she received one particularly "mean" rejection after she had gotten her book deal with Little, Brown. She resisted the urge to send back the letter stapled to an article from *Publishers Weekly* about the lucrative book deal she had won. On reflection, however, Meyer admitted that her query letters were perhaps not that great—it was her first time creating them, after all—and she does not blame agents for rejecting her. None of that mattered in the fall of 2003, however—the Phoenix stay-at-home mom had, against the odds, broken into the New York publishing scene with a major bang.

A LOVE STORY WITH A BITE

On October 5, 2005, *Twilight* was published with an initial print run of 750,000 copies. It immediately shot to the number-five spot on the *New York Times* best sellers list, eventually rising to number one.

The success meant a wave of interviews and book events, which were completely new to Meyer. Unsure what to expect from their new and inexperienced Mormon author, Little, Brown sent a publicist to Arizona—to make sure, as Meyer told *Entertainment Weekly*, "I wasn't wearing a skirt over my jeans or something." She told Seattlepi.com that while she grew more comfortable with readings and signings over time, initially she found them really daunting, and she often vomited when touring to promote her first book.

Meyer's first novel, *Twilight*, was published in 2005 and immediately became a publishing sensation, appealing to readers of all ages around the world.

Meyer need not have been nervous. Her fans and readers embraced her almost immediately. Although Meyer acknowledges that some Mormon readers were surprised to learn that a fellow Mormon would write about vampires, it was the love story rather than the monsters that hooked readers. Meyer's publisher, Little, Brown and Company, emphasized the love story in its catalog copy, calling *Twilight* "deeply romantic and extraordinarily suspenseful." The description focused not on the potential "scary" factor of the vampire tale but on the theme at the heart of the story: "*Twilight* captures the struggle between defying our instincts and satisfying our desires."

A *Publishers Weekly* starred review from July 2005 stated, "The main draw here is Bella's infatuation with outsider Edward, the sense of danger inherent in their love, and Edward's inner struggle— a perfect metaphor for the sexual tension that accompanies adolescence." The review goes on to say that these elements will be familiar to nearly all teens and will keep readers madly flipping through the pages.

That essence was not lost in Meyer's subsequent books. In a 2007 *New York Times* book review, Liesl Schillinger wrote that the Twilight trilogy "seethes with the archetypal tumult of star-crossed passions, in which the supernatural element serves as a heady spice."

BACK TO THE DRAWING BOARD: SEQUELS

Meyer had agreed to a multiple-book deal with her publisher. That meant she wasn't able to kick back, relax, and savor the success of *Twilight* for long. Aside from appearing at press interviews and readings, as well as raising three children, Meyer had sequels to write.

The experience of writing the first sequel was a bit different from writing *Twilight*. Previously she had been writing only for herself. This time, she had an editor and an established fan base. She was now writing for publication and had a reputation to maintain and an audience to please. But since Meyer loves her characters and doesn't take herself too seriously, she was up for the task.

Meyer's writing process was slightly different the second time around. In an interview with William Morris of *A Motley Vision* (http://www.motleyvision. org), a blog dedicated to Mormon arts and culture, Meyer explained that since she was still so new at writing, her process was still evolving. She told Morris she was "lucky *Twilight* wasn't a muddled catastrophe": she began writing it without an outline or a full picture of where she was going with her story. With *Twilight*, she started writing in the middle of her story and continued until the end. Then she went back and wrote the beginning, revising where needed to be sure everything was logically aligned.

With her subsequent books, Meyer decided to be more organized. She still wrote out of sequence— writing what she called the "money" scenes, or the best scenes, first. These scenes were the most fun and the easiest to write, "kind of like eating the ice cream before the broccoli," she told Morris. The finished pieces helped unfold the other scenes, suggesting plot details, dialogue, and twists. This approach also kept Meyer from experiencing so-called writer's block. With her mind full of images and ideas for her story, she would often have four hundred pages of material before she knew it. Then she would set to editing.

Meyer prefers to write in the quiet of the night, alone in her "office," which is a desk in the middle of the house. She edits during the day, when there are too many distractions to immerse herself completely in her story and create new material. For Meyer, editing mostly entails reading the scenes she's put to paper in the night and fine-tuning the transitions and details that connect them. By then she is so close to finishing that even the less exciting parts of the book are a thrill to write.

In order to be a successful author, Meyer has simply cut off some distractions: for example, she no longer watches television programs she used to enjoy. She told Morris that watching television now drives her crazy—she has so much creativity brewing inside her that she just can't sit still and waste her time. She does not read as much as she did before taking up writing, nor is she as dedicated to crafts, such as scrapbooking. She said she has not given up these other hobbies and interests permanently, but for now she is enjoying writing as her main creative outlet.

THE NEW J. K. ROWLING?

After a 2008 event to promote *Breaking Dawn*, Diane Mangan, then director of children's merchandising at Borders, told *Entertainment Weekly*, "I kept saying that there will never be another book in my career like Harry Potter 7. Who would have thought a year later we'd be talking like this again?"

Fans of the Twilight series proudly show their excitement for the stories at book signings and film events around the world. They have been given nicknames such as "twilighters," "twi-hards," and "fanpires."

Almost immediately, the publishing world began comparing Meyer with J. K. Rowling, author of the Harry Potter series. When asked in a 2008 *Time* interview how she felt about the comparisons, Meyer said her feelings were mixed. "On one hand," she said, "it's really flattering. I'm a huge fan. On the other hand, there is a bit of backlash because then people say, 'Who does she think she is?' And then I feel bad, like I'm the one going around and saying this, which I'm not. I don't enjoy that side of it."

There are actually very few similarities between the two authors. It is true that both women had success writing young adult books with otherworldly themes, and that both women seem to have gotten their inspiration from nowhere (Rowling says the idea for Harry Potter "fell into her head" as she was traveling on a train in England). However, Rowling's writing style is completely different from Meyer's. Meyer gets swept up in the emotions of the characters and allows the story to unfold based on what she believes her characters' responses in situations would be. The emotions spill off the page: Bella swoons and gasps, and the work borders on melodrama. Still, the comparisons of the two authors kept coming.

Rene Kirkpatrick, a book buyer at All for Kids, a Seattle-based children's book and music shop, told Seattlepi.com that Meyer was actually becoming bigger than Rowling in some circles. For teenage girls, twelve and older—and often their moms, too—Meyer was a literary pop star.

Meyer does not appear to be intimidated by this development, but she did tell *USA Today* that there will never be another J. K. Rowling and that holding her up to that standard puts a lot of pressure on her. She maintains that she is happy being Stephenie Meyer and that that is "cool enough for her."

HEADING TO THE BIG SCREEN

After the success of *Twilight* in print, it was inevitable that the book and its sequels would be made into films. Meyer was excited to see her books adapted to the big screen. She was eager to see the images that had existed only in her mind and on her pages spring into life. In particular, Meyer was excited to see the meadow scenes in movie form.

In 2005, Meyer told *A Motley Vision*, "I'm a very visual person—when I read a book, I usually cast it in my head as I go. So, long before I knew I was writing a novel, I was already casting my characters." Meyer said she quickly had an image of Edward in her mind as she was writing *Twilight*. When the book was optioned for film, she had very specific ideas about the kind of actor who should portray Edward. It had to be someone truly

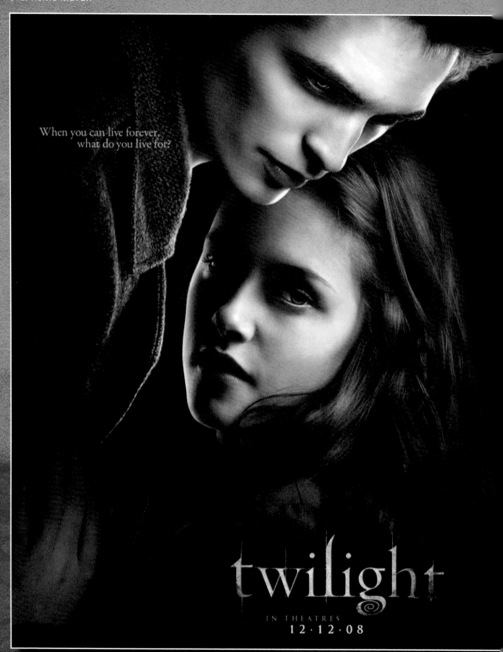

When you can live forever,
what do you live for?

twilight

IN THEATRES
12·12·08

The poster for 2008's *Twilight* movie features the stars, Robert Pattinson and Kristen Stewart. The director consulted with Meyer throughout the making of the film and made no changes to the story without checking with her first.

remarkable and enticing to make the story believable and make readers feel the same love and sense of urgency that Bella does. Before the Twilight films were made, Meyer said that her dream actor to play Edward was Henry Cavill, a British actor. While Cavill would not ultimately play Edward, American audiences have come to know him in his role on the Showtime series *The Tudors*, and he will play Superman in the 2013 film *Man of Steel*.

In the same 2005 interview, Meyer said she was less picky about who would play her book's heroine, Bella. She was adamant only that the actress should not be a Hollywood "it girl," that it should be someone to whom every girl can relate. Meyer believed many contemporary actresses would do a fine job, and she mentioned Emily Browning of *Lemony Snicket* fame. As for directors, Meyer did not express a preference, but said she'd certainly take Steven Spielberg or Ron Howard if she could get them!

THE PATH TO PRODUCTION

The film rights for *Twilight* were originally optioned to MTV Films. For about three years, the film was in development with the studio. Various drafts of the screenplay were written, but they drifted from Meyer's text, and in the end the final draft was very different from the original story.

CRITICISM AND PARENTAL WARNINGS

Stephen King, legendary horror writer and author of books such as *The Shining* and *Christine*, told *USA Weekend* in February 2009: "Both Rowling and Meyer, they're speaking directly to young people… The real difference is that Jo Rowling is a terrific writer and Stephenie Meyer can't write worth a darn. She's not very good." Meyer fans took offense, but his comments do not stray from many of Meyer's own regarding her writing ability. Meyer thinks of herself as a storyteller more than a perfect writer, and she still refers to herself as an "amateur." King did not disparage her for her success, however, and went on to say that her books are successful because they resonate so well with their target audience, especially about love.

Meyer's books have received criticism from some other camps, not for the quality of the writing but for the themes of her stories. Some of the critiques have come from people with a religious perspective. In her book review in *Today's Christian Woman*, Dawn Zemke wrote that Meyer's books should bear a warning label. Zemke claimed that, although Meyer doesn't openly criticize religious faith, vampires and werewolves and other fantastical creatures that appear in her works "carry a mythology regarding life, death, and God that can be at odds with biblical truth."

Bella and Edward do address some difficult questions in their intense discussions over whether Bella should become a vampire to be with Edward forever. They question the nature of good and evil, the possession of souls, and whether vampires hold a place in God's creation.

Others, including Phillip McGraw (best known as television's Dr. Phil), express concern over the very nature of Edward and Bella's relationship, which oversteps love and enters into a dangerous obsession. In an episode of his show about obsessive love, Dr. Phil mentioned that he felt uncomfortable during the scenes in *Twilight* in which Edward watches Bella as she sleeps. A number of feminist writers have expressed similar qualms.

When she reviewed the script, Meyer was concerned. At a press conference in Los Angeles in 2008, Meyer said the script read like a perfectly decent vampire movie, but that it had nothing to do with her story. She worried about the impact it would have if her fans and she herself did not recognize her story in the films.

For a while, the project lingered with MTV Films, but in 2007, Summit Entertainment acquired the rights. This time, Meyer wanted to be sure she protected her story from the outset. She insisted that the writers read the book and stay true to her vampires as they are portrayed in her story. That meant that there would be no fangs and no coffins and that

Meyer chose to base her romantic saga in Forks, Washington, which has very little sunshine and lots of mist and rain—the perfect eerie setting for a vampire story.

the vampires must twin-
kle in the sunlight.

Summit Entertainment
took a different approach
from the previous studio,
one that better aligned
with Meyer's vision.
Rather than change the
story, the studio wanted to
use the film—and subse-
quent films—as vessels to
launch an entire franchise
based on the books, to
create a Twilight "brand."
For this approach to be
successful, the film had to
be a close adaptation of
the book.

Summit, unlike MTV
Films, allowed Meyer to
be a part of the filmmak-
ing process and to weigh
in on any changes that
were made to the story,
no matter how small.
Meyer was thrilled to be
part of the adaptation, and she recalls the experience as a very good one. She told reporters at the

press conference she was careful not to step on anyone's toes—after all, she did not know how to make a movie—but she contributed ideas and found that the people involved were receptive and interested. She reviewed the script and filled it with red marks, citing places where characters were acting unlike she thought they would or when a scene just felt out of place. Meyer told reporters that about 90 percent of her ideas were incorporated into the film.

Five years after *Twilight* was first born, the thirty-four-year-old Meyer was a *New York Times* best-selling author and a multimillionaire. With the August 2008 publication of the final installment, *Breaking Dawn*, there was little time for fans to mourn the end of the story before they had a chance to relive it all again from the start: the *Twilight* movie was released on November 21, 2008. It earned mixed reviews by critics, but fans were hooked all over again.

LIFE AFTER TWILIGHT

W hen the final book was published, a new wave of Twilight fanaticism was just beginning. With the release of the Twilight Saga movies—*Twilight* (2008), *New Moon* (2009), *Eclipse* (2010), *Breaking Dawn Part I* (2011), and *Breaking Dawn Part II* (due for release in 2012)—the series broadened its audience and rekindled the enthusiasm of existing fans.

The films made stars of their actors, Kristen Stewart (Bella), Robert Pattinson (Edward), and Taylor Lautner (Jacob). Fans launched worldwide "Team Edward" and "Team Jacob" campaigns. ("Team Edward" represents Twilight fans who think Bella should be with Edward, and "Team Jacob" includes those who think she should choose Jacob.) There has been a surge

Although Meyer has stayed remarkably down-to-earth in spite of her massive success, her family now enjoys this large home in Cave Creek, Arizona, a desert town outside Phoenix.

of merchandising around the world, from jewelry to action figures.

Meyer's publicist, Elizabeth Eulberg, was promoted to the position of director of global publicity for Stephenie Meyer. This means she manages planet Earth's insatiable demand for the Twilight mega-author. The books have been life- and career-changing for many readers, publishers, moviemakers, and actors. How has all this fame and fortune changed Meyer's own life?

LIFESTYLE OF THE RICH AND FAMOUS

Meyer says the success of the Twilight books has changed her routine in some ways—it now involves book events, press appointments, and writing—yet she remains fundamentally the same down-to-earth person as ever. Speaking to *USA Today* in 2008, Meyer explained that, after thirty years of being a "normal" person, it's hard to lose your moorings.

Having a firm foundation in her family and faith, Meyer is not easily tempted by the downsides of money and recognition. Most of the time, she said, she is home with her husband and children, and that's just where she prefers to be. Her newfound wealth, however, has meant that Meyer's husband has been able to leave his job and become a

In North Brunswick, New Jersey, Twilight fans turned out for a midnight prom-themed release party celebrating the publication of *Breaking Dawn* on August 1, 2008.

full-time stay-at-home dad. So this literary superstar has managed to turn her good fortune into a means of keeping her family close together.

Being a generous and caring person, Meyer is extremely grateful to her fans for their support. She feels a sense of responsibility to them—and tries to reflect this in the way she shows appreciation to them at readings and through letters. Regarding the plots of her books, however, she told *USA Today* there is no way to please everyone, so she has to follow her own instincts.

Meyer did find keeping up with fan mail to be quite a chore initially—the letters arrive in swarms. In 2008, she told *Newsweek* that she was fighting the urge to hire an assistant to help her manage all the mail. She eventually did decide to hire an assistant, and one of the person's first tasks was to get the bins and bins of fan mail under control. Still, she is a very hands-on person, and she likes to be in touch with fans. She told *Newsweek* she would like to sit down and write everyone a three-page letter but simply doesn't have the time. There is one rule that Meyer is set on: any fan mail that comes to her unlisted home address is immediately thrown away. Her privacy is sacrosanct.

Reading events have grown exponentially since Meyer's career first began. On the release date of *Breaking Dawn*, more than 1,500 bookstores stayed open after midnight to host release parties. Meyer limited her appearances to bookstores and venues that could hold literally thousands of fans. Tickets to such events from New York to Los Angeles were sold out in less than an hour. Meyer's sister Emily told Karen Valby of *Entertainment Weekly* that she could recall readings where they could only hope for about twenty people to show up. She said, "It would be me and my five little friends, because of course I loaned out my books and got my whole neighborhood reading, and we'd go to the ice cream store, and she'd read." She went on to say that those were the events that Meyer truly loved.

During a tour through Volterra, Italy, where parts of *New Moon* take place, more than six hundred European fans arrived to be part of the celebration.

This trip was followed by a book-signing "prom" at the Arizona State University gymnasium, an event that drew one thousand fans. Meyer adored the event, as she loves to dress up and had been crushed to learn that people in the New York publishing world don't traipse around in ball gowns. She arrived at the "prom" in a burgundy wedding dress adorned with sequins, looking every bit the prom queen.

CASTING CALL

A film based on Meyer's first adult novel, *The Host,* was rumored to be in preproduction as of summer 2011. According to a casting call Web site (http://www.acting-auditions.org), auditions were planned for roles such as Melanie Stryder and Jared Howe, and filming was scheduled to begin in September 2011. Producers Nick Wechsler, Steve Schwartz, and Paula Mae Schwartz acquired the rights to adapt the book to film. The film is said to be the first part of a trilogy, with sequels *The Soul* and *The Seeker* to follow. In an interview with Larry Carroll of MTV Networks, Meyer shared her actor wish list for the film, including such Hollywood stars as Robert Redford, Ben Affleck, and Matt Damon. This represents a departure from her desire for the Twilight stars to be up-and-coming, relatively unknown talents. With *The Host* trilogy, Meyer told Carroll, she could envision the actors being big names.

MIDNIGHT SUN

Coming off the thrill and excitement of book events, Meyer could not wait to return home to Arizona and get back to what she loves most: writing books. With the Twilight series complete, Meyer was ready to move on—almost. She began writing the Twilight story from a different point of view, this time from that of Edward. As Meyer explains on her Web site, the book, *Midnight Sun*, began as an "exercise in character development that got wildly out of hand."

Meyer reread the first chapter of *Twilight* and considered how differently all of its experiences were for Edward. The book is told from Bella's point of view, and all she knew early on is that a gorgeous, mysterious boy was looking at her. It was Edward who would be feeling more complex emotions at that stage in the story, and Meyer wanted to explore that.

It wasn't long before Meyer was hooked. She felt compelled to know more about Edward's experiences in Alaska, during his time away from Forks and Bella. Meyer was

The popularity of Meyer's books has extended far beyond the United States. Eager fans arrive at the Champs-Élysées Virgin Megastore in Paris, France, for the launch of *The Short Second Life of Bree Tanner* on June 5, 2010.

really pleased with the way the book was shaping up. She found that Edward—a careful character, one who overthinks everything—had a fascinating story to tell. It was also a long story to tell—at not even halfway through, Meyer had more than three hundred pages of material.

On her Web site StephenieMeyer.com, Meyer wrote that her mother was initially skeptical of the project, but upon reading some of the manuscript became a big supporter. The author said she could easily see *Midnight Sun* on the shelves as part of the other books in the saga.

Meyer's enthusiasm was cut promptly short when one early draft of the *Midnight Sun* manuscript was leaked in full on the Internet. There is a downside to having such a large fan base: you are ever in demand by millions of hungry fans eager to know what happens next and unable to wait until the work is finished. The manuscript spread like wildfire across the Internet without Meyer's or her publisher's permission or knowledge.

On hearing the news, Meyer stopped the project immediately, making this announcement on her Web site in August 2008:

So where does this leave Midnight Sun? *My first feeling was that there was no way to continue. Writing isn't like math; in math, two plus two always equals four no matter what your mood is like. With writing, the way you feel changes everything. If I tried to write* Midnight Sun *now, in my current frame of mind, James would probably win and all the Cullens would die, which wouldn't dovetail too well with the original story. In any case, I feel too sad about what has happened to continue working on* Midnight Sun, *and so it is on hold indefinitely.*

OTHER PROJECTS

Stepping away from Forks and her beloved vampires, Meyer wrote her first adult novel, *The Host*, which was published in 2008. This work of science fiction tells the story of an alien invasion with a romantic twist. An Amazon Best of the Month review stated, "Those wary of sci-fi or teen angst will be pleasantly surprised by this mature and imaginative thriller, propelled by equal parts action and emotion."

But Meyer couldn't stay away from vampires for long. On December 13, 2010, Meyer's publisher announced in a press release that Meyer would be releasing a new novella as part of the Twilight series. The book tells the story of a newborn vampire who appeared in *Eclipse*. It became available in bookstores and by electronic download on June 5, 2010.

Robert Pattinson, Kristen Stewart, Stephenie Meyer, and Taylor Lautner attend the actors' handprint ceremony at Grauman's Chinese Theatre in Hollywood in November 2011. The Twilight movies brought Meyer's characters to life and have made international stars of their young actors.

The book, *The Short Second Life of Bree Tanner*, got mixed reviews, but with such avid fans behind her, the reviews really didn't matter. Monica Hesse of the *Washington Post* probably said it best in her book review: "The satisfaction of *Twilight* novels cannot be measured by such terms as 'good' and 'bad.' This goes double for 'Bree,' which… all fans will read and all haters will skip regardless of the reviews."

The spell cast by the Twilight series shows no sign of lifting. In April 2011, Little, Brown and Company published *The Twilight Saga: The Official Illustrated Guide*. As part of the book's release, the publisher held a competition to select the biggest Twilight fans from the United States, Brazil, China, France, Germany, Italy, Mexico, Taiwan, and the United Kingdom. The winners attended a special international fan event that included extended time interviewing the author.

What Meyer will do next is anybody's guess. She is dedicated to the craft of writing and her imagination works overtime, so fans can expect her to keep dreaming up and sharing stories for a long time to come. Meyer shares her new ideas and projects on her Web site, and she continues to love hearing from her fans.

ON STEPHENIE MEYER

Birth date: December 24, 1973

Birthplace: Hartford, Connecticut

Parents: Stephen and Candy Morgan

Siblings: Seth, Emily, Jacob, Paul, and Heidi

Childhood home: Phoenix, Arizona

Currently resides: Cave Creek, Arizona

Schooling: Chaparral High School in Scottsdale, Arizona; Brigham Young University in Provo, Utah, where she received a B.A. in English in 1995

Religion: Meyer was raised a Mormon, and she continues to belong to the church.

Work history: Before becoming an author, Meyer worked briefly as a receptionist.

Marital history: Married Christiaan "Pancho" Meyer in 1994

Children: Three sons—Gabe, Seth, and Eli

Favorite authors: Jane Austen, Orson Scott Card, L. M. Montgomery, Maeve Binchy, and William Shakespeare

Hobbies: Aside from writing, Meyer enjoys reading, scrapbooking, making costumes, and spending time with her husband and sons.

Inspiration: A dream inspired her first book, *Twilight*, which earned Meyer a three-book publishing deal in 2003.

Interesting facts: Bella was the name Meyer had chosen for the daughter she never had. She doesn't watch vampire movies (other than the Twilight films).

81

Achievements: Meyer was the biggest selling author of the years 2008 and 2009. Meyer sold about 29 million books in 2008 and more than 27 million books in 2009 (those numbers include her adult title, *The Host*). In 2008, the four books in the Twilight series claimed the top four spots on *USA Today*'s year-end best sellers list, making Meyer the first author ever to achieve this feat (which she repeated the following year). By August 2009, Meyer had broken J. K. Rowling's record on *USA Today*'s best sellers list; the four Twilight books had spent fifty-two straight weeks in the top ten.

Honors: In 2009, Meyer was ranked number five on *Forbes*' list of Hollywood's Top-Earning Women. She was the only author on the list. The same year, she was ranked number 82 on *Vanity Fair*'s list of the Top 100 Information Age Powers. *Forbes* named Meyer one of the Ten Most Powerful Women Authors in 2011.

ON STEPHENIE MEYER'S WORK

The books in the Twilight series have been an incredible success story. The books have sold more than one hundred million copies worldwide. Translation rights have been sold in nearly fifty countries. The sales figures below are drawn from reports in *Publishers Weekly*.

Twilight. New York, NY: Little, Brown and Company, 2005.

First printing: *Twilight* had an initial print run of seventy-five thousand copies.

Sales: A month after its release, *Twilight* reached the number-five position on the *New York Times* best sellers list (children's trade books), and it later hit number one.

Awards and honors: *Publishers Weekly* Best Book of the Year (2005), *New York Times* Editor's Choice (2005), *Teen People* Hot List Pick, American Library Association (ALA) Top Ten Best Books for Young Adults, Amazon Best Book of the Decade So Far, *Publishers Weekly* Kids' Book Adults Would Love

New Moon. New York, NY: Little, Brown and Company, 2006.

First printing: *New Moon* had an initial print run of one hundred thousand copies.

Sales: The book spent more than twenty-five weeks at the number-one position on the *New York Times* best sellers list. In 2008, it was the biggest-selling children's paperback book, selling more than 5.3 million copies. In 2009, the paperback sold another 4.5 million copies.

Awards: Pacific Northwest Library Association Young Readers Choice Award (2009)

Eclipse. New York, NY: Little, Brown and Company, 2007.

First printing: *Eclipse* had a first printing of one million copies, ten times the initial run of *New Moon*.

Sales: Readers bought 150,000 copies of *Eclipse* in its first twenty-four hours on sale. The hardcover book sold more than 1.1 million copies in 2007. In 2008, *Eclipse* was the best-selling backlist (previously released) children's hardcover book, selling more than 4.5 million copies. In 2009, it was the best-selling children's paperback book, selling more than 2.5 million copies.

Awards and honors: Colorado Blue Spruce Young Adult Book Award (2009), *New York Times* Editor's Choice (2007)

Breaking Dawn. New York, NY: Little, Brown and Company, 2008.

First printing: Book four in the series was published with an initial print run of 3.2 million copies, the largest in the company's history.

Sales: On the first day of the book's release, 1.3 million copies were sold. *Breaking Dawn* was the best-selling new children's hardcover book of 2008, selling more than 6 million copies. In 2009, it took the top spot for children's hardcover backlist (previously released) titles, selling more than 4.6 million copies. In 2010, it was the top selling children's e-book, and it sold more than one million copies in paperback that year.

Awards: Children's Choice Book Awards Teen Choice Book of the Year (2009), Galaxy British Book Awards WHSmith Children's Book of the Year (2009)

The Host: A Novel. New York, NY: Little, Brown and Company, 2008.

First printing: The first printing for *The Host*, Meyer's first adult book, was 750,000 copies.

Sales: The novel sold 1.2 million copies in 2008 and another 912,000 copies in 2009. The book reached number one on the *New York Times* best sellers list for fiction.

Awards and honors: The book was named on Amazon's Best of the Month list for May 2008.

The Short Second Life of Bree Tanner: An Eclipse Novella. New York, NY: Little, Brown and Company, 2010.

First printing: The book had a first printing of 1.5 million copies.

Sales: The novella sold more than 2.2 million copies in hardcover in 2010.

Interesting facts: One dollar for each book sold in the United States from the first printing was donated to the American Red Cross International Response Fund, which supports disaster relief efforts. It was also made available as a free e-book just two days after its publication.

Twilight (2005)

"Isabella Swan, 17, narrates this riveting first novel, propelled by suspense and romance in equal parts…The main draw here is Bella's infatuation with outsider Edward, the sense of danger inherent in their love, and Edward's inner struggle—a perfect metaphor for the sexual tension that accompanies adolescence. These will be familiar to nearly every teen, and will keep readers madly flipping the pages of Meyer's tantalizing debut."—*Publishers Weekly*, October 2005

New Moon (2006)

"Meyer's narrative is heavier on teen drama than supernatural activity, yet perhaps that's what has made her tales such must-haves for young readers. *New Moon* piles on the suspense and romance, but if it's blood-sucking one craves, you won't find it here."—*USA Today*, September 27, 2006

Eclipse (2007)

"Meyer's trilogy seethes with the archetypal tumult of star-crossed passions, in which the supernatural element serves as heady spice. As Bella and her vampire swain channel Romeo and

Juliet, Heathcliff and Cathy, their audience falls under the spell of a love that is not only undying, but undead." — *New York Times*, August 12, 2007

Breaking Dawn (2008)
"Edward and Bella's romance, while sweet on paper, is viewed through rose-colored, love-conquers-all glasses that ignore some harsh realities. Their desperation to constantly be together sometimes feels more like obsession than love.

Like its predecessors, *Dawn* has sold millions of copies. Whether you find its story disturbing or thought-provoking, one thing is certain: your daughter, her friend (or perhaps even your friend!) is likely to have read it." — *Today's Christian Woman*, November 1, 2008

The Short Second Life of Bree Tanner (2008)
"Meyer's talents lie not in filling in her characters' backgrounds but in maintaining them in a constant state of exquisite torment. Intelligent and gifted, Bella, Jacob and Edward are intrinsically glamorous to readers. But Bree is PVT (poor vampire trash) and she knows it. Unqualified to even understand her situation, much less change

it, she inspires empathy in the reader, but not a whole lot of anticipation." — *Salon*, June 8, 2010

The Host (2010)

"As in her Twilight series, Meyer is more interested in relationships than in flashy genre conventions. Will the survivors believe Wanderer when she says that she's joined forces with Melanie's brain — or will they shoot her on sight? The answers are slow in coming, despite the author's well-intentioned ruminations on desire and the kindness of strangers. *The Host* starts rolling again in its last hundred pages and Meyer's affirmative life lesson is disarming. If only the rest of the book had as much soul." — *Entertainment Weekly*, May 2, 2008

December 24, 1973 Stephenie Morgan is born in Hartford, Connecticut; her family moves to Arizona.

1994 Stephenie Morgan and Christiaan "Pancho" Meyer marry.

1995 Meyer receives a B.A. in English from Brigham Young University.

1999 Meyer gives birth to her first son. She decides not to pursue an earlier dream of law school to stay home and raise her child.

June 2, 2003 Meyer has a dream about a girl and a vampire in a meadow. She begins frantically typing what will become chapter 13 of *Twilight*.

August 2003 Meyer begins submitting query letters to literary agents with little expectation of success.

October 2003 Meyer signs with her top-choice agency, Writers House.

November 2003 Meyer signs a $750,000, three-book deal with Little, Brown and Company.

October 5, 2005 *Twilight* is published.

August 21, 2006 *New Moon*, the second book in the Twilight series, is published.

April 2007 Summit Entertainment options the rights for the film version of *Twilight*.

August 7, 2007 *Eclipse*, the third book in the saga, is published; subsequently, the first three Twilight books spend a combined 143 weeks on the *New York Times* best sellers list.

May 6, 2008 Little, Brown publishes Meyer's first adult book, the science-fiction romantic thriller *The Host*.

August 2, 2008 *Breaking Dawn* is published. Released at 12:01 AM, 1.3 million copies are purchased in its first twenty-four hours on sale.

August 28, 2008 Meyer announces she is ending work on *Midnight Sun* after early drafts of the manuscript are released without permission on the Internet.

November 21, 2008 The movie version of *Twilight* is released in the United States.

June 5, 2010 Meyer publishes *The Short Second Life of Bree Tanner*.

2011 Meyer signs on to be a producer of adaptations of *The Host* and Shannon Hale's *Austenland*, the latter as part of Fickle Fish Films, which Meyer created along with Meghan Hibbett.

GLOSSARY

ADAPTATION The conversion of a story from a novel into the plot of a film.

ADVANCE Payment that an author receives from a publisher to write a book.

AGENT A person whose job it is to scout literary talent and find editors to publish authors' works.

ANATHEMA A person or thing that is strongly disliked.

ANGST A feeling of anxiety, dread, or anguish.

ARCHETYPAL Constantly recurring as a character type, symbol, or image in literature.

ARID Very dry.

BOOK DEAL The agreement between an author and a publisher, often brokered by an agent.

BOOK SIGNING An event at which an author appears to read and sign copies of his or her book.

DRAFT The first version of a complete manuscript, which is edited and revised before publication.

EDITOR The person who works with an author on revising and improving a manuscript to prepare it for publication.

EXPONENTIALLY Very rapidly; literally, if something's rate of change must be expressed using exponents.

FICTION Written works that are not based on facts or actual people or events; invented stories.

FILM DIRECTOR The person who guides actors in the making of a film and who makes all the major decisions about the script, scenes, and execution of a film.

FILM RIGHTS An agreement in which a studio buys the right to adapt a novel into a film.

FRANCHISE A film that is or has the potential to be part of a series and lends itself to merchandising.

GENRE A category or type of fiction, such as mystery, romance, or horror.

INSATIABLE Impossible to satisfy.

MANICALLY In a wildly excited, energetic, or emotional manner.

MANUSCRIPT A complete book or collection of stories that has not yet been published.

MELODRAMA A work marked by exaggerated action, conflict, and emotion.

MERCHANDISING The activity of trying to sell products by advertising or displaying them in an appealing manner; also, selling products that are related to something (such as a book, TV show, movie, or sports team) in order to make more money.

MISSIONARY A person who goes to a foreign country to do religious work, such as converting others to one's religious beliefs, educating people, or helping the poor.

MOORING An established practice or stabilizing influence.

MORMON A member of the Church of Jesus Christ of Latter-day Saints, a church founded by Joseph Smith in 1830. Members accept the Book of Mormon as holy scripture.

NEUROTIC Unusually anxious, fearful, or depressed.

NOVELLA A story that is longer and more complex than a short story but not as long and complex as a novel; a short novel.

OPTION To get the exclusive right to use an author's work as the basis for a movie.

PREPRODUCTION The process of preparing a film for production, including such steps as casting, choosing locations, and designing costumes and sets.

PRINT RUN The number of copies of a book that are printed.

PROTAGONIST The main character in a literary work.

PUBLICIST The person whose job it is to promote a book and its author to increase visibility, press coverage, and sales.

PUBLICITY The process or business of attracting public attention to a person, product, cause, etc., often by providing information with news value to the media.

PUBLISHER The person who decides which books should be published; also, a publisher is a company that publishes books.

QUERY A letter that an author writes to pitch a book idea to an agent or publishing house.

READERSHIP The group of people who read the work of a particular author or publication.

REJECTION LETTER A letter from an agent or publisher that lets an author know his or her work will not be represented or published.

REVIEW An article in print or online in which the writer rates a book or otherwise judges its quality.

SACROSANCT Most sacred; inviolable.

SCRIPT The written version of a movie, including all dialogue and basic set direction.

STRAITLACED Very strict or proper in conduct and beliefs.

TARGET AUDIENCE The intended audience for a book; the audience for which the book will be marketed.

WRITER'S BLOCK A usually temporary condition in which a writer is unable to continue with a piece.

WRITER'S WORKSHOP A class or gathering in which a writer's work is critiqued.

YOUNG ADULT (YA) A term used by publishers for teen readers.

Alliance for Young Artists & Writers
557 Broadway
New York, NY 10012
(212) 343-6493
Web site: http://www.artandwriting.org
This nonprofit organization identifies teens with excep-
tional artistic and literary talent and brings their
work to a national audience through the
Scholastic Art & Writing Awards. Started in 1923,
the awards provide an opportunity for American
and Canadian students to be recognized for their
talents and gain financial assistance for their
education and development.

Canadian Library Association (CLA)
1150 Morrison Drive, Suite 400
Ottawa, ON K2H 8S9
Canada
(613) 232-9625
Web site: http://www.cla.ca
The Canadian Library Association is an award-winning,
not-for-profit organization that serves as the
national voice of the Canadian library and information community.

Children's Book Council (CBC)
54 West 39th Street, 14th Floor
New York, NY 10018
(212) 966-1990
Web site: http://www.cbcbooks.org

A nonprofit trade association for children's trade book publishers, the CBC works on reading lists to help teachers, librarians, parents, and booksellers discover new, wonderful books for children and teens. The CBC is also a cosponsor of the Children's Choice Book Awards, the only national child-selected awards program.

Hachette Book Group USA
Little, Brown Books for Young Readers
237 Park Avenue
New York, NY 10017
(212) 364-1200
Web site: http://www.hachettebookgroup.com
Hachette Book Group is a leading U.S. trade publisher headquartered in New York. Fans of Stephenie Meyer can learn more about her books on the company's Web site and send fan mail to Meyer in care of Little, Brown Books for Young Readers.

International Reading Association (IRA)
800 Barksdale Road
P.O. Box 8139
Newark, DE 19714-8139
(800) 336-7323
Web site: http://www.reading.org
The IRA is a nonprofit, global network of individuals and institutions committed to worldwide literacy. The association promotes high levels of literacy for all by improving the quality of reading instruction,

advancing research, and encouraging a lifetime reading habit.

National Council of Teachers of English (NCTE)
1111 W. Kenyon Road
Urbana, IL 61801-1096
(217) 328-3870
Web site: http://www.ncte.org
The National Council of Teachers of English is devoted to improving the teaching and learning of English and the language arts at all levels of education. Its mission is to promote the development of literacy and the use of language to construct personal and public worlds and to achieve full participation in society.

Publishers Weekly
71 West 23rd Street, #1608
New York, NY 10010
(212) 377-5500
Web site: http://www.publishersweekly.com
Publishers Weekly is the book industry's leading news magazine, covering every aspect of creating, producing, marketing, and selling the written word. It provides book and media reviews, bestseller lists, interviews with top authors and publishers, and business news, including trends and developments in the industry.

Society of Children's Book Writers and Illustrators
8271 Beverly Boulevard
Los Angeles, CA 90048

(323) 782-1010

Web site: http://www.scbwi.org

The SCBWI is a professional organization for individuals writing and illustrating for children and young adults in the fields of children's literature, magazines, film, television, and multimedia.

Women's National Book Association (WNBA)

P.O. Box 237, FDR Station

New York, NY 10150

Web site: http://www.wnba-books.org

The Women's National Book Association is a national organization of women and men who work with and value books. WNBA exists to promote reading and to support the role of women in the community of the book.

WEB SITES

Due to the changing nature of Internet links, Rosen Publishing has developed an online list of Web sites related to the subject of this book. This site is updated regularly. Please use this link to access the list:

http://www.rosenlinks.com/AAA/Meyer

Albert, Lisa Rondinelli. *Stephenie Meyer: Author of the* Twilight *Saga* (Authors Teens Love). Berkeley Heights, NJ: Enslow Publishers, 2009.

Beahm, George W. *Bedazzled: Stephenie Meyer and the* Twilight *Phenomenon*. Nevada City, CA: Underwood Books, 2009.

Bringle, Jennifer. *Vampires in Film and Television* (Vampires). New York, NY: Rosen Central, 2012.

Brooks, Riley. *Edward or Jacob? Quick Quizzes for Fans of the* Twilight *Saga*. New York, NY: Scholastic, 2010.

Clarke, Amy M., and Marijane Osborn, eds. *The* Twilight *Mystique: Critical Essays on the Novels and Films*. Jefferson, NC: McFarland & Co., 2010.

Cook, Chris. *Twilight Territory: A Fan's Guide to Forks and LaPush*. Sequim, WA: Olympic View Publishing, 2009.

Gresh, Lois H. *The Twilight Companion: The Unauthorized Guide to the Series*. New York, NY: St. Martin's Griffin, 2008.

Hardwicke, Catherine. Twilight: *Director's Notebook: The Story of How We Made the Movie Based on the Novel by Stephenie Meyer*. New York, NY: Little, Brown and Company, 2009.

Heos, Bridget. *Vampires in Literature* (Vampires). New York, NY: Rosen Central, 2012.

Hopkins, Ellen, and Leah Wilson. *A New Dawn: Your Favorite Authors on Stephenie Meyer's Twilight Series*. Ann Arbor, MI: Borders, 2008.

Kim, Young, and Stephenie Meyer. *Twilight: The Graphic Novel, Volume 1* (Twilight Saga). New York, NY: Yen Press, 2010.

Krohn, Katherine E. *Stephenie Meyer: Dreaming of Twilight* (USA Today Lifeline Biographies). Minneapolis, MN: Twenty-First Century Books, 2011.

Meyer, Stephenie. *Breaking Dawn*. New York, NY: Little, Brown and Company, 2008.

Meyer, Stephenie. *Eclipse*. New York, NY: Little, Brown and Company, 2007.

Meyer, Stephenie. *The Host: A Novel*. New York, NY: Little, Brown and Company, 2008.

Meyer, Stephenie. *New Moon*. New York, NY: Little, Brown and Company, 2006.

Meyer, Stephenie. *The Short Second Life of Bree Tanner: An Eclipse Novella*. New York, NY: Little, Brown and Company, 2010.

Meyer, Stephenie. *Twilight*. New York, NY: Little, Brown and Company, 2005.

Meyer, Stephenie. *The Twilight Saga: The Official Illustrated Guide*. New York, NY: Little, Brown and Company, 2011.

Navarre, Sam. *Vampires in America* (America's Supernatural Secrets). New York, NY: Rosen Central, 2012.

Orr, Tamra. *Stephenie Meyer* (Blue Banner Biography). Hockessin, DE: Mitchell Lane Publishers, 2010.

Reagin, Nancy Ruth. *Twilight and History*. Hoboken, NJ: John Wiley & Sons, 2010.

Shapiro, Marc. *Stephenie Meyer: The Unauthorized Biography of the Creator of the Twilight Saga*. New York, NY: St. Martin's Griffin, 2009.

Sheen, Barbara. *Stephenie Meyer: Twilight Saga Author* (Innovators). Detroit, MI: KidHaven Press, 2010.

Spencer, Liv. *Love Bites: The Unofficial Saga of Twilight*. Toronto, ON, Canada: ECW Press, 2010.

Stewart, Sheila. *The Psychology of Our Dark Side: Humans' Love Affair with Vampires & Werewolves* (The Making of a Monster: Vampires & Werewolves). Broomall, PA: Mason Crest Publishers, 2011.

Vaz, Mark Cotta. *Twilight: The Complete Illustrated Movie Companion*. New York, NY: Little, Brown and Company, 2008.

Woog, Adam. *Vampires in the Movies* (The Vampire Library). San Diego, CA: ReferencePoint Press, Inc., 2011.

Associated Newspapers, Ltd. "Twilight Fan, 49, Gets Robert Pattinson and Kristen Stewart Inked Over Whole Back." *Daily Mail*, January 5, 2011. Retrieved August 15, 2011 (http://www.dailymail.co.uk/news/article-1344355/Twilight-fan-49-gets-Robert-Pattinson-Kristen-Stewart-inked-WHOLE-back.html).

Baptiste, Tracey. *Stephenie Meyer* (Who Wrote That?) New York, NY: Chelsea House, 2010.

Bidisha. "Twilight's Feminist Backlash." *Guardian*, July 15, 2010. Retrieved July 20, 2011 (http://www.guardian.co.uk/commentisfree/2010/jul/15/twilight-feminist-backlash-bella).

Carroll, Larry. "'Twilight' Writer Stephenie Meyer Wants Matt Damon for 'Host' Movie, Discusses Her Rabid Fanbase—MTV Movie News." MTV.com, April 9, 2008. Retrieved August 1, 2011 (http://www.mtv.com/news/articles/1585112/twilight-writer-stephenie-meyer-wants-matt-damon-host-movie.jhtml).

Cox, David. "Twilight: The Franchise That Ate Feminism." *Guardian*, July 12, 2010. Retrieved July 25, 2011 (http://www.guardian.co.uk/film/filmblog/2010/jul/12/twilight-eclipse-feminism).

David, Avril. "The 10 Most Powerful Women Authors." *Forbes*, June 6, 2011. Retrieved July 5, 2011 (http://blogs.forbes.com/avrildavid/2011/06/06/the-10-most-powerful-wom-authors).

Elgin, Susan. "The Secret Life of Vampires." *Newsweek*, July 26, 2008. Retrieved July 13, 2011 (http://

www.thedailybeast.com/newsweek/2008/07/25/
the-secret-life-of-vampires.html).

Futterman, Erica. "'Twilight' Author Stephenie Meyer
on Her Musical Muses, Upcoming Movie and
Mermaid Dreams." *Rolling Stone*, August 8,
2008. Retrieved July 15, 2011 (http://www.
rollingstone.com/music/news/twilight-author-
stephenie-meyer-on-her-musical-muses-
upcoming-movie-and-mermaid-
dreams-20080808).

Giles, Jeff. "Book Review: *The Host*." *Entertainment
Weekly*, May 2, 2008. Retrieved June 30, 2011
(http://www.ew.com/ew/article/0,,20308569_
20197308,00.html).

Goodnow, Cecelia. "Stephenie Meyer's Forks-Based
Saga of Teen Vampire Love Is Now a Global Hit."
Seattlepi.com, August 6, 2007. Retrieved June
29, 2011 (http://www.seattlepi.com/ae/books/
article/Stephenie-Meyer-s-Forks-based-saga-of-
teen-1245825.php).

Goodnow, Cecelia. "'Twilight' Author's Teen Fans
Have True Love Flowing Through Their Veins."
Seattlepi.com, June 28, 2006. Retrieved
August 2, 2011 (http://www.seattlepi.com/
ae/books/article/Twilight-author-s-teen-fans-
have-true-love-1207451.php).

Grossman, Lev. "Stephenie Meyer: A New J. K.
Rowling?" *Time*, April 24, 2008. Retrieved August
4, 2011 (http://www.time.com/time/magazine/
article/0,9171,1734838,00.html).

Hesse, Monica. "'The Short Second Life of Bree Tanner,' Stephenie Meyer's 'Twilight' Novella, Reviewed." *Washington Post*, June 6, 2010. Retrieved July 25, 2011 (http://www.washingtonpost.com/wp-dyn/content/article/2010/06/05/AR2010060502251.html).

Kirschling, Gregory. "Stephenie Meyer's 'Twilight' Zone." *Entertainment Weekly*, July 5, 2008. Retrieved August 12, 2011 (http://www.ew.com/ew/article/0,,20049578,00.html).

Laing, Olivia. "Stephenie Meyer—A Squeaky-Clean Vampire Queen." *Observer*, November 14, 2009. Retrieved July 5, 2011 (http://www.guardian.co.uk/books/2009/nov/15/profile-stephenie-meyer-vampire-queen).

Memmott, Carol. "'Twilight' Author Stephenie Meyer Unfazed as Fame Dawns." *USA Today*, August 1, 2008. Retrieved July 20, 2011 (http://www.usatoday.com/life/books/news/2008-07-30-stephenie-meyer-main_N.htm).

Meyer, Stephenie. "Stephenie Meyer." Goodreads.com. Retrieved July 5, 2011 (http://www.goodreads.com/author/show/941441.Stephenie_Meyer).

Meyer, Stephenie. "Twilight Series—*New Moon*—The Story." StephenieMeyer.com. Retrieved July 10, 2011(http://www.stepheniemeyer.com/nm_thestory.html).

Meyer, Stephenie. "Twilight Series—*Twilight*—FAQ." StephenieMeyer.com. Retrieved July 5, 2011 (http://www.stepheniemeyer.com/twilight_faq.html).

Morris, William. "Interview: *Twilight* Author Stephenie Meyer."*A Motley Vision* blog, October 26, 2005. Retrieved July 20, 2011 (http://www.motleyvision.org/2005/interview-twilight-author-stephanie-meyer).

Murray, Rebecca. "Stephenie Meyer 'Twilight' Interview—Stephenie Meyer on 'Twilight' the Movie." About.com. Retrieved August 6, 2011 (http://movies.about.com/od/twilight/a/stephenie-meyer_5.htm).

PublishersWeekly.com. "Stephenie Meyer by the Numbers." *Publishers Weekly,* May 12, 2008. Retrieved December 1, 2011 (http://www.publishersweekly.com/pw/print/20080512/2898-stephenie-meyer-by-the-numbers-.html).

Roback, Diane. "Bestselling Children's Books 2008: Meyer's Deep Run." *Publishers Weekly,* March 23, 2009. Retrieved December 1, 2011 (http://www.publishersweekly.com/pw/by-topic/childrens/childrens-book-news/article/5252-bestselling-children-s-books-2008-meyer--s-deep-run-.html).

Roback, Diane. "Farewell to Harry." *Publishers Weekly,* March 24, 2008. Retrieved December 1, 2011 (http://www.publishersweekly.com/pw/by-topic/childrens/childrens-book-news/article/17591-farewell-to-harry-.html).

Roback, Diane. "Franchises Flying High: Children's Books: Facts & Figures 2010." *Publishers Weekly,* March 21, 2011. Retrieved December 1, 2011

(http://www.publishersweekly.com/pw/by-topic/
childrens/childrens-book-news/article/46543-
franchises-flying-high-children-s-books-facts--
figures-2010.html).

Roback, Diane. "The Reign Continues." *Publishers
Weekly*, March 22, 2010. Retrieved August 15,
2011 (http://www.publishersweekly.com/pw/
by-topic/childrens/childrens-book-news/article/
42533-children-s-bestsellers-2009-the-reign-
continues.html).

Rosman, Katherine. "The Death of the Slush Pile."
Wall Street Journal, January 22, 2010. Retrieved
July 7, 2011 (http://online.wsj.com/article/
SB10001424052748703414504575001271351
446274.html).

Schillinger, Liesl. "Children's Books/Young Adult—
Books—Review—*Eclipse*." *New York Times*,
August 12, 2007. Retrieved July 9, 2011 (http://
www.nytimes.com/2007/08/12/books/review/
Schillinger7-t.html).

Skurnick, Lizzie. "'*Short Second Life of Bree Tanner*':
Stephenie Meyer Slays Her Own Vampires."
Salon, June 8, 2010. Retrieved July 25, 2011
(http://www.salon.com/books/review/2010/06/08/
short_life_bree_tanner).

Smith, Cynthia Leitich. "Author Interview: Stephenie
Meyer on Twilight." *Cynsations* blog, March
27, 2006. Retrieved July 19, 2011(http://
cynthialeitichsmith.blogspot.com/2006/03/
author-interview-stephenie-meyer-on.html).

Sullivan, Robert. "Stephenie Meyer: Dreamcatcher."
    Vogue, March 3, 2009. Retrieved July 15, 2011
    (http://www.vogue.com/magazine/article/
    stephenie-meyer-dreamcatcher).

Time, Inc. "10 Questions for Stephenie Meyer." *Time*,
    August 21, 2008. Retrieved August 2, 2011
    (http://www.time.com/time/magazine/article/
    0,9171,1834663,00.html).

Truitt, Brian. "Exclusive: Stephen King on J. K.
    Rowling, Stephenie Meyer." *USA Weekend*,
    February 2, 2009. Retrieved August 12, 2011
    (http://whosnews.usaweekend.com/2009/
    02/exclusive-stephen-king-on-jk-rowling-
    stephenie-meyer).

Valby, Karen. "Stephenie Meyer: Inside the 'Twilight'
    Saga." *Entertainment Weekly*, July 31, 2008.
    Retrieved July 10, 2011 (www.ew.com/ew/
    article/0,,20308569_20211938,00.html).

Wloszczyna, Susan. "Classic Romantic Triangle
    Takes Monstrous Form in 'New Moon.'" *USA
    Today*, November 20, 2009. Retrieved July
    20, 2011 (http://www.usatoday.com/life/
    movies/news/2009-11-13-newmoon13_
    CV_N.htm).

Zemke, Dawn. "'Breaking Dawn' by Stephenie Meyer."
    Today's Christian Woman, Vol. 30, Issue 6,
    November 1, 2008, p. 10. IB_Groupon_Final.pdf.

INDEX

ABOUT THE AUTHOR

Tracy Brown is the author of young adult biographies on subjects as diverse as Missy Elliot and Babe Ruth, and has also acted as a compilation editor for nonfiction titles.

Brown is the former executive editor of Breakthrough to Literacy, a McGraw-Hill Education early literacy program, and has written and contributed fiction, nonfiction, and poetry passages to several K–12 study guides and test preparation manuals.

Brown holds a B.S. in journalism from Emerson College and an M.A. in European history from the University of Amsterdam. She currently lives in the Netherlands.

PHOTO CREDITS